FRAGMENTS OF A MOSAIC

Lisa Basnight Reid

Fragments Of A Mosaic
Copyright © 2018 Lisa Basnight Reid

All rights reserved. No part of this book may be used or reproduced by any means, graphic, electronic, or mechanical, including photocopying, recording, taping or by any information storage retrieval system, without the written permission of the publisher except in the case of brief quotations embodied in critical articles and reviews.

Entegrity Choice Publishing
PO Box 453
Powder Springs, GA 30127
info@entegritypublishing.com

The views expressed in this work are solely those of the author and do not necessarily reflect the views of the publisher, and the publisher hereby disclaims any responsibility for them.

All of the characters, names, incidents, organizations and dialogue in this novel are either products of the author's imagination or are used fictitiously.

Book Cover Designed by:
Kylie Dayton

ISBN: 978-0-9991780-6-5
Library of Congress Control Number: 2018930040

Printed in the United States of America

Dedication

This book is dedicated to all women who have felt alone, worthless, empty, and inadequate at some point in their lifetime. You are worthy, you are beautiful, you are unique, you are more than enough, you are magnificent in your own right, and you are extraordinary. It is my prayer that my story will encourage you to look up to where your help comes from – from the Lord. And if you do not know Him, I pray by the end of one of these chapters, you will give your heart to Him to mend, heal, and restore. All you have to do is ask Him and believe.

Acknowledgements

I could not have written this book without the love of my life, my husband Dexter. Not only is he my biggest cheerleader, he is also my biggest support. No matter what I endeavor to do, he is the one to encourage me. I am the luckiest woman on the planet because he is my husband. He truly is the best gift God has given to me. I love him with all my heart and always will.

To Christine Bloodworth, I thank you. Without you, I would never had met my publisher. It was at the Women Can Conquer Conference that not only did I meet you, but I also met Roxie! Whether you know it or not, that day changed my life. It was meant for me to be there, to worship with you, and to connect with other like-minded women.

To my publisher, Roxie, thank you so much for your patience. I appreciate that more than you know. I'm so blessed to have met you and to be working with you on this project.

To my sister friends who have encouraged me along the way to write this book, I salute you... Carolyn-Renee Murray, Phyllis Clark, Cordelia Manuel, Simone Richards, and Maggie Lloyd – my sister circle. I love you all so very dearly; may our circle never be broken. To Yolanda Dupree, Denise Henry, Kathi Byrd, and Earnestine Jones...you are like little gift wrapped presents with beautifully tied bows. You adorn my life and I am so grateful for you.

To Babbie Mason, thank you for your encouragement and for your prayer at The Inner Circle, October 2017. It was the push I needed to finish my book and to sing my song. Thank you for your mentorship and for sharing with me.

To my sister-in-love, Allison, there isn't a book with enough pages to express how much you mean to me, sisters we will always be. Thank you, thank you, thank you for ALWAYS being there, for ALWAYS being willing to listen and never allowing a harsh word to escape your mouth toward me. There is a special crown for you in heaven, and we know why!

You are all "fragments of my mosaic." - Thank You.

Contents

Dedication 3
Acknowledgements 5
Introduction 9

Chapter 1
   I Come from Good Stuff 13

Chapter 2
   The Lost Teenager 17

Chapter 3
   The Single Mother 21

Chapter 4
   The Rape Victim 29

Chapter 5
   The Ex-Wife 35

Chapter 6
   The Care Taker 39

Chapter 7
   The Mother of an Addicted Child 43

Chapter 8
   From Mosaic to Masterpiece 53

Chapter 9
   The Mortar, My Worship 59

Introduction

This book is for women from different walks of life. We are special creatures. Women are strong, sturdy, resilient, and beautiful. Yet we are soft, sensitive, silent, and fragile at times. There is no other being on Earth like a woman.

I wrote this book because of who we are. We are unique in that we can do many things and carry loads that we feel were not meant for us. We are married mothers, single mothers, wives, care-takers, creators, designers, innovators, problem solvers, and so much more. We can also become lost, overwhelmed, disheartened, and unacknowledged.

This book is meant to encourage you, to let you know that you are not alone, to build you up and increase your faith in God.

I am a Masterpiece, created specifically for the only true and living God. So are you. He chose me to bring Him glory. He chose you too. No matter what I have experienced in my life, it will all be for His benefit. It's what I was created for. You were created for the same thing. We may have different gifts, talents, and mindsets, but we all were created for Him. We are daughters of Zion. We are set-apart. We are His.

As you read this book, you will find that my problems get smaller and smaller because my focus on God gets bigger and bigger. Worship and God's Word have been my anchor throughout the disenfranchisements of my life. They will also carry you through any encounter you may face. Think of the weight of what you are going through. God specifically allowed those trials and troubles in your life because He wants you to bring that level of Glory to Him.

There are scriptures after each chapter that have been engraved in my heart. I have referenced them-- sometimes more than once. Use these scriptures and apply them to your life. Pray them out loud so the enemy and his forces can tremble. The word of God in your mouth is a sword, a weapon for an already awesome woman of God – You. (Zechariah 9:13)

So stand up! Be confident! Don't take stuff lying down! You can handle anything that gets thrown your way. Are you going to wimp out, cry and complain and pity yourself OR are you going to face your adversity with grace, with power, with confidence? Give all of your problems to The One who solves them. Put the enemy on notice; his time of running your life is over.

Mosaic: Montage, assortment, mixture, variety, medley

Fragment: Piece, portion, part, scrap, section, bit

My mosaic is:

- ♥ A montage of scraps – the hard things I would rather throw away that have taught me life lessons.
- ♥ Parts of a mixture – the good and the bad, and the ugly, an "up-sized" combo that molded my life.
- ♥ Many bits of variety – colorful fragments, plain fragments, bold fragments, and subdued fragments combined to make art.

♥ More than a few pieces of a medley – put together with mortar that created flair, beauty and an example.

1

I Come from Good Stuff

My father was a preacher, a pastor by the nature of his heart. He was a construction worker by trade. He was a retired military man, a husband and father and friend to many, many people.

He possessed many talents and was crafty with his hands. One that I admired most was his ability to play the trombone. He never had a lesson in his life, but he played it like a master trombonist. He played it passionately and his music was enjoyed by all who would listen.

I thought my Dad could do anything. He could fix stuff. He could sing. He had the most beautiful cursive I've ever seen from a man with just an 8th grade education. He could build things. He even made the walkway, front porch, and backyard patio of our house out of gorgeous multi-colored slate. He had help from a friend, but they did it. I remember him fondly growing up on Pennsylvania Avenue in Mount Vernon, NY.

Daddy never met a stranger. He made a friend everywhere he went. The love of God was so bright in his life that it was almost blinding. I often wondered – "What in the world is he so happy about all the time?" It was God.

When he passed away, people came from all over the East Coast to pay their respects to him and our family. What a rich life he had. The joy of the Lord was definitely his strength.

I had troubles in my first marriage as many couples do. I called my Dad. I wanted the pity, the "it's going to be okay, Baby Girl" encouragement. I was in my 30s and you would think I would be beyond that. I wasn't.

Well, I started with the tears and the complaining, the whining, looking for my father to beat up the big bad husband of mine. That's not what I got.

My father said to me "Tam-Pooh," that's what he used to call me (my middle name is Taamel). He said, "God must think a great deal of you to allow you to go through so much." What? Huh? In my immaturity, I didn't want to hear that! I didn't want philosophy. I didn't want a sermon. I wanted my Dad's ear, his arms around me, and his voice telling me it was going to be okay. I told him, "Dad, I'm not hearing that. That's not what I wanted you to say." He told me that was all he had. It's funny now when I think about it, but it sure wasn't funny back then.

I was upset with my Dad. I forgave him later, though. This book will explain how those "fragments," those things that God allowed me to go through taught me the meaning of what my Dad said and just how valuable I am to God. You are valuable to God as well.

My mother was Wonder Woman. Good Lord, I can't imagine how she did it all. She was a teacher, the greatest cook of all time, mother of six, a grandmother of many, a pastor's wife, a mentor, a Sunday School teacher, a sister and a friend. Every night, she fixed dinner for her family and we ate at the table for every meal. She had a beautiful singing voice. I can still remember singing, "There is No One to Compare with Jesus." I tell you, she was a wonder.

She wore a dress hat to church, even her casual hats looked dressy. When I was in school, she would make her own clothes. Mommy was "famous" for her cooking, but she was known for her homemade rolls. It was a recipe she created herself and passed down to me. Out of the four girls, I was the one who learned to make them. She made them religiously every weekend. We had them for breakfast before Sunday School and we had them for Sunday dinners – faithfully, every Sunday.

I come from good stock, not perfect stock. I come from the stuff that good people are made from. I loved my parents and always will love them. One day, I will see them again.

2

The Lost Teenager

I was in 9th grade taking Advanced English and Advanced Math. In math, I was a grade ahead taking Geometry. It was hard and I had a teacher who was monotone in her speaking. She had impeccable penmanship and I could read her notes on the board very easily – anyone could – but the class was boring.

I fell asleep in class a lot, often missing crucial explanations of theorems and equations. I failed her class and had to take Geometry again during the summer. My best friend failed too, so we had that class in summer school together. My mom wasn't too happy about that. Mother was a Home Economics teacher at my high school. Yep! That was like hell on Earth to a teenager.

In summer school, we had a great teacher who was outgoing, funny, and kept your attention in class. She explained things in great detail and both my friend and I passed the class and the NY State exam. We stood at her window of the school and she would hold her fingers to let us know our final grade. I got an 85% and my friend received an 88%. We were ecstatic and ran to my house to tell my mother. When we got there to tell her, all she said to me was, "Why didn't you get an 88?" It still pinches my heart just to recall it all. My friend took that as a cue to say goodbye and she went home. I just went upstairs to my room and cried. This was one of those times when I felt inadequate, felt that I could not please my mother.

One of my older sisters was there when it happened, and I guess she said something to my mother. I never mentioned it to her. Mommy came upstairs to my room and told me that I had done a good job and she gave me a "pat" hug. It wasn't very convincing. It was as if she didn't want to admit that I had done a good job with something that was difficult for me. That was how I perceived it.

As a 14-year-old kid, I didn't know any better. But for quite some time, I did feel that I could never meet my mother's expectations - ever. All I felt I could do was to fill her expectations of disappointment. I lived most of my adult life trying to measure up, trying to be what she wanted me to be. I failed miserably. To this day, I can only remember my mother telling me that she was proud of me one time. I was a grown woman then and didn't really believe her. It shocked me to hear her say it. But that was a lie. I know my mother loved me, but at that time, negative words had seeped into my innermost being. It was a trick that taunted me for many years of my life. I lived by accepting things that I should have rejected, believing what was said. Then it was quite obvious that I was unhappy, battered and unable to weather the storms of my life. I believed that I wasn't worth very much at all.

It is my prayer for you that the words you speak be acceptable in the sight of God. May your heartfelt thoughts be good and may you quickly turn away from speaking negative or evil things to your children, to your spouse, to your co-workers, or to yourself. May you pleasingly present yourself to God as He has created you.

> *"Even before He made the world, God loved us (me) and chose us (me) in Christ to be holy and without fault in His eyes."*
> *Ephesians 1:4 (NLT)*

> *"In the same way, I will not cause pain without allowing something new to be born, says the Lord."*
> *Isaiah 66:9 (NCV)*

*"Let the words of my mouth be acceptable in Thy sigh,
Oh Lord, my strength and my redeemer."
Psalm 19:14 (KJV)*

3
The Single Mother

My husband and I, from time to time, stay in bed a little longer on Saturdays. We mainly like to chat, laugh, and catch up from the week. But sometimes we talk about how we grew up and discuss things that happened to us as kids.

One Saturday, we talked about my being a single mother. I was pregnant with my oldest child at 16. Church was a big part of my life then and still is today. But it was a lot different in the 1980s. There were "protocols" and "rules" that should not have been broken. Being a pregnant unwed daughter of a pastor was something that was definitely frowned upon. I lived in Mount Vernon, NY – a small suburban city that is only four square miles. Word travelled quickly, and it didn't take long before everyone knew that I was with child and unmarried.

As I mentioned in the previous chapter, I was a very unhappy teenager. I felt unaccepted, uncared for, and out of place. Though my siblings would say that I was spoiled, I felt alone. I imagine a lot of teenage girls have felt this way. My mother had me when she was 43 years old, so there was a huge generation gap there. We did not communicate well at all. We bumped heads a lot, and unsurprisingly, I lost the battles and was always looking for comfort or a way out.

At the age of 15, I was taking quite a few business classes in high school. One of the classes was typing, and I was the fastest typist in my class. One day my teacher requested that I stay behind after class to ask me if I was interested in a job. A city lawyer was looking for a part-time clerk-typist, and my teacher had told him about me. I interviewed just before school let out for the summer and was offered the job. If everything worked out, I would be able to keep that job and eventually work full time. I couldn't wait to tell my mom and dad. They were happy for me and "encouraged" me not to mess it up. I loved this job, and for a girl at age 15, I was able to have my own "little" money. But it was all short-lived.

I sought comfort from the captain of the football team who was a senior. That was not accepted at all by my parents. Of course, I was forbidden to see him any time outside of school, and of course as a teenager, I rebelled, lied, and saw him anyway. When I told my two older sisters that I thought I was pregnant, they did not say a single negative word to me, not a one. I didn't appreciate that then; I sure do now. My second oldest sister took me to Planned Parenthood to get a pregnancy test – very discreetly and confidentially. It was confirmed then. She was with me when I told my mother. That was the hardest thing I ever had to do in my life. I expected her to say all that she did, and it wasn't pretty. In fact, it was awful. You can probably imagine what was said. I was a slut, a tramp, and a whore. She even said I forced my boyfriend to have sex with me. My father wasn't there at the time, so I had to break the news twice, and telling my father wasn't any easier. He told me right then that he knew he didn't have to save any money for me to go to college. The money that he had saved, he spent. Needless to say, if I didn't feel bad about myself already, that experience would have sealed my fate.

I grew up in a Pentecostal church, so when you were "caught" in sin, you were chastised pretty severely. I was made to confess my sin before the church and ask forgiveness. It was a pivotal time in my life. Of course, I didn't see it like that. But if I had not gone through all of this, I would not have known later on in life just how much God loves me. He cares so much for his sheep.

He must have thought a great deal about me to allow me to go through so much at age 16. Just writing this makes me say, "Wow!" I am so blessed.

My mother told me that no one would ever love me with a child. I believed her. In the hospital, in recovery, my mother told the nurse that I would be back with another child. I was going to be just like all of the other unwed mothers. But I am here to tell you that I am not a statistic. Those words spoken over me were crushed when I accepted Christ as my Savior. Those words where broken when I began to declare the goodness of God over my life.

You have control over what is spoken over you if you have the Word of God in your heart. God loved me and my son. He was not illegitimate in the eyes of God. And I was not a number. God knows the exact number of hairs on my head. He knew me then, and he knows me know. God doesn't make mistakes, even though we tend to make many of them in life. I encourage you to read the Word of God, research and find what He really thinks about you. Declare THOSE words as the ones that define your life and witness the negative words be cancelled in the mighty name of Jesus! I hope my story brings healing to you, so that God can receive the glory He so deserves.

It was an extremely hard time in my life and my pregnancy was stressful. I left my little clerking job at the attorney's office. My typing teacher had thought I would be a good fit for the job, and even though I was happy to have it, I still felt inadequate. I felt hated by everyone and I thought, surely, my boss wouldn't want me pregnant and working there. I allowed the words and opinions of others to mold my future. Later, I learned that they really cared about me and they really liked me. I didn't see that at the time because I couldn't see past how I felt about myself. They told me later that I could have stayed and everything would have worked out. My thoughts of myself sabotaged a good thing.

Eventually, it was my son and me against the world. We kept each other together. We showed each other the love we both needed. We laughed and watched cartoons together. My son loved Ghostbusters, so we played that a lot. I was "slimed" quite a bit. He was always "Winston" and I was always some kind of ghost that needed to be caught. We appreciated the little things and had fun together, but there were many challenges to face. I can remember not having much to eat. One dinner consisted of frozen corn, rice, and ketchup. I didn't make a big deal of it and as a matter of fact, my son loved rice and corn, but it hurt not to be able to feed him how I wanted to. We had picnics on the living room floor of our apartment in Mount Vernon. He didn't know anything was wrong. He loved me anyway and never complained about not having enough to eat. He was such a good boy and never gave me an ounce of trouble. God made him like that, and I believe He gave him to me as a gift to get through the hard times that were coming.

I had a hard time finding and keeping a job. I was on public assistance but never wanted to stay on it; I was on a mission to secure gainful employment. I applied for a job at the Mount Vernon Hospital Methadone Maintenance Treatment Center as a clerk/typist. The interview went well, and I was offered the job. It was my experience in the lawyer's office that impressed them so much. Things were looking up for us, but I was still young, broken, hurting, and lost.

Almost two years later, I decided to move south. I wanted a better life for my son. Life in New York was hard, and I wanted him to be able to ride his tricycle without having to get on a bus to get to a park. I wanted something better. But before I did that, I met a gentleman who worked for Planned Parenthood. He was a friend of my boss at the hospital and was hosting a support group for pregnant teens. He asked me to speak to them, but I, of course, didn't think I was qualified. I didn't think much of myself at all. But I agreed and I told them my story.

I told those teen girls that I was 16 when I got pregnant and I disappointed my family. I told them I gave up my hopes of going to college and that my parents gave up too. I told them I was on public assistance and it was hard to feed my son. I told them how I felt about myself and it wasn't good. But I also told them that I graduated from high school early with a B+ average and that I had a good job with the hospital and had received a promotion in less than a year because I found $225k had been embezzled from the program. Things changed and I resigned. I told them that I was moving to Atlanta in hopes of a better life for my son. And I did.

I had no idea at that time what God was putting inside me. I wanted to help those girls. After all that I had gone through, He put in my heart the desire to speak life into teenage girls and unwed mothers. But if I had not had my son and experienced those hardships, how could I have spoken to those girls? If I could speak to those pregnant girls now that I'm in my 50s, I would say this:

- God doesn't make wimps.
- You are priceless.

- You are a beast!
- You are unique.
- You are handcrafted.
- You are the daughter of God.
- You have a big brother who won't let you be bullied.
- You have untapped power.
- You have unused gifts.
- You have underutilized talents.
- You do measure up.
- You are enough.

"Even before he made the world, God loved us (me) and chose us (me) in Christ to be holy and without fault in his eyes."
Ephesians 1:4 (NLT)

"We can rejoice, too, when we run into problems and trials, for we know that they help us develop endurance. And endurance develops strength of character, and character strengthens our confident hope of salvation. And this hope will not lead to disappointment. For we know how dearly God loves us, because he has given us the Holy Spirit to fill our hearts with is love."
Roman 5:3-5 (NLT)

"Don't copy the behavior and customs of this world, but let God transform you into a new person by changing the way you think. Then you will learn to know God's will for you, which is good and pleasing and perfect."
Romans 12:2 (NLT)

"For we are God's masterpiece. He has created us anew in Christ Jesus, so we can do the good things he planned for us long ago."
Ephesians 2:10 (NLT)

"Thank you for making me so wonderfully complex! Your workmanship is marvelous—how well I know it."
Psalm 139:14 (NLT)

"In the same way, I will not cause pain without allowing something new to be born, says the Lord."
Isaiah 66:9 (NCV)

"And the very hairs on your head are all numbers. So don't be afraid; you are more valuable to God than a whole flock of sparrows."
Luke 12:7 (NLT)

"Death and life are in the power of the tongue."
Proverbs 18:21 (KJV)

4
The Rape Victim

I moved to Atlanta from New York in the fall of 1987. I was 21 years old with a 3-year-old son, no job, and no place to call my own. I stayed with my cousin until I could find work and a place to stay. After three months of searching, I found a job and moved into my own apartment. It didn't take me long to get used to being on my own, even if I struggled to take care of myself and my son. It was just the two of us, and I was fine with that. We didn't have any furniture, not even a bed. Drawing strength from one another, we persevered, and I got him settled into a day care – The Love Bug Learning Center. I remember it like it was yesterday. I look back on those days with a certain degree of amazement, especially in light of how my son's life has unfolded. He is now 34 years old, a Lieutenant, a County Fire Marshall, and a professional wrestler.

Getting through day-to-day life in that sparsely furnished apartment was a challenge, but nothing could compare to what came next. I never experienced crime in New York. When I moved to Atlanta, however, all of that would change. I was 21, sheltered, and immature. I trusted most anyone. I needed to get my utilities turned on, and I was waiting at the bus stop to go to City Hall. I had no idea where I was going. A man drove up in a city vehicle, so I thought it was safe to take a ride from him. He took me to get my utilities on, and we even had lunch together. He didn't take me back to where he picked me up from. He took me to an isolated park and I was raped at knife point.

Without being too graphic, I was choked and beaten, but I was able to get away. I had no idea where I was and I had to find my way back to my son's day care and home. I was bloodied and tried to hide it as best I could. The looks and stares from those on the bus weren't enough to make me run, but it was enough to make me feel shameful. I didn't call the police for fear they would blame me – after all, I did get in the car with a stranger. The words my mother said to me when I told her I was pregnant echoed in my ears. I heard them over and over again in my mind. They tormented me for weeks and months and years, thereafter. So, I didn't tell my parents – I felt they would have just told me that I had asked for it. I told no one until later in life. A rape is traumatic for anyone. It was no exception for me. To this day, I can remember my assailant's scent, his name, what he was wearing and what he looked like.

As a child, I grew accustomed to not expressing my feelings. I was never allowed to. So as an adult, I suppressed my feelings about the rape and kept them hidden inside for many years. You see, I didn't think much of myself anyway. I was the youngest of six and never felt that I could measure up. I couldn't please my mother; I had disappointed her over and over, and she made sure I knew it; and I had my son out of wedlock. I was a total embarrassment to my parents and a hopeless mess. The words that were spoken about me and my son were life changing for the worse. I believed it all and I lived it for most of my adult life. Words are powerful. This is one of the reasons why I am writing this book. I hope you will understand that you can reverse the negative words directed toward you. You can break the curses that are cast over your life.

It was only through my relationship with Christ that I was able to change the way I thought of myself. I went to a church in Decatur, GA – Chapel Hill Harvester Church. As the pastor was speaking, he paused in the middle of his message. I will never forget these words. He said, "There is a young woman here and she is sitting over here (meaning in the section I was sitting in). The Lord wants you to know that you are loved more than you know and you are bigger than you have been made to think you are. You have been forgiven, now you have to forgive yourself." He saw me weep. And those who were around me were instructed to "love" on me. That was the beginning of the change in my life.

As the fragments of my mosaic were coming together in my life, in time, I began to speak positive words, to declare all the good that God had intended for me and to mute the negative words and thoughts that plagued me for most of my life. I don't blame my mother; I don't blame my father. They were good parents even with their mistakes.

If they were alive today, they would be as loving as they could be. All of those thoughts were from the enemy. He was trying to kill me from the inside out. But it was the Word of God that spoke life where I thought there was none. As I grew in my relationship with God, I realized I was able to withstand so much because He was protecting me. He was watching me. He was strengthening me. He was establishing me.

- I am a daughter of a King.
- My brother is the heir to the highest throne in all of the universe.
- I was created for a purpose – to worship the Lord of all.
- I am a masterpiece made up of fragments of a mosaic.
- I am beautiful.
- I am smart.
- I am creative.
- I am fun to be around.
- I am loved.

"But the Lord is faithful, and he will strengthen you and protect you from the evil one."
II Thessalonians 3:3 (NIV)

"The tongue can bring death or life; those who love to talk will reap the consequences."
Proverbs 18:21 (NLT)

"In the same way, I will not cause pain without allowing something new to be born, says the Lord."
Isaiah 66:9 (NCV)

5

The Ex-Wife

In September 2016, my ex-husband had a massive stroke. This was the kind of stroke that a 70 or 80 year-old person would have. His girlfriend found him on the floor of their apartment; she got him to the hospital in time, but he was in very bad shape.

My youngest son, my daughter, and I rushed to the hospital as soon as we could. It took a while for us to get some answers, but we eventually learned that their dad had been admitted to a critical care unit for stroke victims.

Heavily medicated and groggy, he could only open his eyes for moments at a time. Only two of us at a time were allowed in the room to visit. I sat with him, tearing up as I looked at this man whom I knew to be difficult, opinionated, stubborn, and sometimes very mean. I prayed for him and he reached for my hand. He knew I was there, even though he was fading in and out. He would wake up and squeeze my hand tightly, not letting it go. Eventually, I told him to rest and assured him that I would be back to see him later so he would let go of my hand. I kissed him on the forehead, and my daughter and I walked back to the waiting area in tears.

There was a lot of swelling on his brain, and for someone his age, 53, that was extremely dangerous and drew much concern from the doctors and neurologists. Talk of surgery, opening his skull to allow for swelling, and the lasting effects was frightening to us all. We didn't know if he was going to make it, but we prayed. We asked our friends to pray. We asked our church to pray. We believed God would hear our prayers and we trusted God.

It was hard for my grown children to see their father in that condition. It was particularly hard for my daughter, who was 21 at the time and his next of kin. She would be the one to give the doctors, neurologists, and surgeon's permission to do what was needed. I knew she had no idea what was coming. I just had to be there for her.

My ex-husband lost mobility on his entire left side. He could not recognize anything on the left of him – not even his own arm, leg, or foot. The doctors called it "neglect." It was going to be a long road of recovery for him and my daughter had to see him through it. Along with holding down a job and school full-time, she became her father's primary care taker.

My youngest son said to me, "Mom, you are the best ex-wife ever." I told him that it was the love of Christ inside of me that allows me to have kindness towards him. We had a rocky marriage with lots of anger, mental and physical abuse, dire financial issues, and emotional infidelity. Yes, there is such a thing as emotional infidelity. My ex-husband chose to spend a great deal of time with another married woman who was close to me.

We did not like each other. There was no romance in our marriage, no vacations, no time together, no time alone with one another. He often talked negatively about me and laughed at me from time to time about the way I dressed. We did not cultivate our marriage. It withered away. Some very hurtful words were said to me, words that I will never forget. But those times are a reminder of God's grace in my life, how he carried me through that marriage. My kids saw the worst side of their father many, many times. He was often very physical with my youngest son. Though it took some time for me to forgive during our marriage, forgiveness came through our divorce. I can now say that I hold no grudges and I am at peace.

Do you have the will power within you to forgive those who have hurt you? If your total freedom were at stake, would you forgive? Choosing NOT to forgive can kill you, physically and emotionally.

"Then you (I) will experience God's peace, which exceeds anything we (I) can understand. His peace will guard your (my) hearts and minds as you (I) live in Christ Jesus."
Philippians 4:7 (NLT)

"Therefore, humble yourselves under the mighty hand of God, that He may exalt you in due time, casting all your cares upon Him, for He cares for you."
I Peter 5:6-7 (NKJV)

6

The Care Taker

My husband was stuck on the stair lift one Saturday evening in December 2016. The lift just stopped – with him on it. He couldn't move. I was deeply concerned and wondered what I was going to do. My first impulse was to call my son who was at a worship conference a couple hours away. He knew all the ins and outs of that lift and how to fix its quirks. I called him and attempted every fix he suggested, but nothing worked. At this point, I had no choice but to call 911. Firemen came, three of them. They were perplexed after resetting the fuse box, trying to figure out how to carry this 6'8", handicapped man up five more steps. Finally, the solution was revealed! There was a reset button on the lift that was in an odd place – very easy to overlook – and they got him upstairs.

The next day was Sunday. When I got to church, I had a melt-down in my car, right there in the parking lot. The weight of being a care giver is enormous and I have found it to be unbearable at times. But I cried and I moved on. After all, I am a strong woman and I keep things moving. I obviously needed that little bit of a release.

About a week later, in my monthly women's meeting, the Lord whispered some very sweet words of encouragement. He said "I hear you, I saw your tears – they are like prayers, I keep them all and I have not forgotten you. See? I care for you." WOW... I wept again as I shared this with the ladies.

> *"You keep track of all my sorrows.*
> *You have collected all my tears in your bottle.*
> *You have recorded each one in your book."*
> *Psalm 56:8 (NLT)*

This is another example of God's love for us. He cares so much that he concerns Himself with every one of our tears. He made us special and He cares for us especially.

I was a care taker once before for my mother. She had dementia and Alzheimer's disease. It was hard to see my mother in that state. She was always very independent, strong and strong willed. She had a stroke a few years after my father passed, and her health seemed to deteriorate from there.

At first she lived with my brother and his family for a couple of years. It got to be too much for them. Really, Mommy needed her daughters to take care of her. She came to live with me, my ex-husband and our kids for a little while – about 8 months – until my oldest sister could retire and take care of her. Mommy was a handful. She needed a lot of attention and she offended her home health nurse, Sharon, many times, but Sharon took it in stride, realizing that this is not who Mommy really was, but that this disease can sometimes bring out the worst in people. My mother often accused Sharon of stealing her beloved Wedgewood pieces from London. There were times I cried often. It was difficult to distinguish between the mother I depended on before and the mother that depended on me at that time.

On many occasions, Mommy would get up in the middle of the night. I had bells on her door and on the bathroom door so I could hear her. She wandered sometimes. She loved to watch DVDs before bed, especially Jennifer Lopez in "Enough"... She screamed at the same points in the movie every time she watched it no matter how many times she watched it. She loved watching Tyler Perry/Madea movies too. Sometimes, she would wake up my kids to change the DVD for her – in the middle of the night. They had to get up early to get to school the next morning, but they were troopers. My daughter didn't mind at all. She loved her grandma. Sleep disruptions are common amongst Alzheimer's patients.

This time was particularly difficult on us all. My mother's moods would change often and would not be pleasant most times. Sometimes Mommy could be found staring at nothing in particular. She never wanted to live with me in the first place and often threatened that she was going to leave. She would demand that I take her to the "old folk's home," and she would pack her own bag to let me know she was serious. In her bag would be a wig, one shoe, one slipper, her adult diapers, and she would put on her coat wearing her other pair of slippers. Usually I would just procrastinate and tell her (calmly) that I would take her wherever she needed to go, but I had to feed the children first, or I would have to give them their baths first or something so time would pass. She would calm down by then and usually tell me that she was happy I was taking care of her and that she was sorry. She really didn't want to go to the old folk's home and I didn't want her to go there either.

Those were the times that were hardest. Those were the times that I needed a hug. I was married to my ex-husband at the time and that didn't happen, but my sweetie pie kids loved on me. They were God's hug for me.

Mommy passed away in September of 2007, just after her 84th birthday. All of us miss her, our Mommy.

7

The Mother of an Addicted Child

On Thanksgiving of 2014, my 16-year-old son came home high. He had been smoking marijuana. He was acting very strangely as marijuana is a "downer". My son couldn't sit still; he was very agitated and could not calm himself down. My youngest son is usually the one who would, for the most part, tell the truth. All teenagers lie at some point, but my buddy would usually cave in and tell the story. So it was no surprise when he told me that he was smoking marijuana in the basement. It was a surprise that he did it, but not a surprise that he told me. He was still acting very odd. After a little time passed, I called my brothers and sisters and they began to pray.

Dexter and I prayed through my son's room and we prayed through the house all night. There was something wrong with our son. He was doing things that didn't make sense. He would take a gum wrapper, take my hand and place the gum wrapper in my hand and then close my hand. He got a pencil, opened my hand and put the pencil in my hand. He took a baseball cap and put it on my head – each one at a time. He also just wouldn't go to sleep. It was all very strange and concerning…

My brother told me that if he was not better in the morning, I should take him to the ER. That's what we did. They immediately put him in a protective ward. I thought, "Dear God, what is happening?" His blood tests came back positive for marijuana but nothing else. I called his father and he came immediately. As a mother, lots of things were going through my mind… "Is my baby losing his mind? Am I losing my mind? I cannot put my son in an institution. Where did I go wrong? Am I not a good mother?" I could go on and on with the thoughts.

My ex-husband offered to stay with our son. I had been up for two days – in the hospital for almost 24 hours. The hospital had done all they could and was looking for a rehabilitation place for our son. It was Thanksgiving weekend, so nothing was open. So we went home to get some rest. I knew he would be alright if his father were there.

I called the hospital a few hours later and my son had been transferred to a psychiatric hospital. What? His father had signed the papers and did not call me. I was furious. I was so angry. We had joint custody of our kids, but I had physical custody, so nothing should have been done without my consent. I was not thinking about the goodness of God at that moment. When I say, however, it was God that kept me, that was the truth. I had a few choice words for my ex-husband who always wanted to control things, but I reserved those choice words for another time.

We could only see our son on visitation days, and the first one was a couple of days away. I made it there and saw my son. He was wearing clothes that were so small, he couldn't button them and we couldn't bring him anything. He begged me to take him home; my baby was only 16. He was going through withdrawal from the marijuana for sure, but he was still acting abnormally. This was a mother's nightmare, the darkest time of my life. To see your child in the care of strangers and those strangers telling you that you couldn't see him but two times per week was absolutely unnerving. I knew something was wrong with my son; he was not crazy. Something was wrong.

Before we left, I made sure that the hospital knew that I had physical custody of our son, and that under any circumstances, no decisions are to be made without my consent or I would sue. I was very clear and direct.

That evening, I got a call from the doctor at the psychiatric hospital. They wanted to give our son a small dose of Ritalin. I consented because I knew he was a handful, 260 pounds and 6'1". He kept us up for two days. The next morning, I received another phone call from that same doctor. Our son had suffered a seizure and was foaming at the mouth. He was rushed to Children's Hospital in Atlanta.

I dropped everything and got to the hospital as soon as I could. When I did, my son recognized me and hugged me for dear life. He begged me to take him home. I couldn't. We needed to get to the bottom of this. There was something wrong and we needed to know what was going on. All kinds of tests were taken, EKGs, CAT scans, Spinal Tap, EEGs to detect seizures. They poked and took ungodly amounts of blood from him. And he was still acting unlike himself.

My son was belligerent. He was disrespectful. He was vulgar. He complained that his head hurt often. He would hold his head telling the voices to stop. He would be talking to "people" who weren't in the room. He was a big 16-year-old with strength to pick me up and throw me around. His father could handle him much better than I could and he had to. Our son had lost knowledge of simple things. He couldn't remember his sister's name. He couldn't remember my name. He knew I was Mom, but couldn't remember that my name was Lisa. He called my husband "Pops." He remembered that. In his room, I wrote the following scriptures on the white board.

> *"No weapon formed against you shall prosper..."*
> *Isaiah 54:17 (NLT)*

> *"Even when I walk through the darkest valley, I will not be afraid, for You are close beside me."*
> *Psalms 23:4 (NLT)*

My son would get up out of bed and take his finger and erase those scriptures from the board. That was confirmation that my son was being attacked by the enemy, from the pit of hell and I was not having it. I went into "Mama Mode" and resolved to go to war on behalf of my son. I declared that my son was going to live and not die. I declared God's promise that my children and my children's children and my children's children's children would receive salvation and they would be saved. I was not going to let the enemy have my son. I continued to pray but I primarily worshipped. I am a worshipper at heart. My church prayed, my family and friends prayed and I prayed, but I worshipped through all of it. I knew that the enemy could not stay where there was worship. My worship to the Most High God and the King of Kings became my faith lifter, my strength builder, my confidence!

The Lord sent a pediatric neurologist to evaluate him, and she diagnosed him with Acute Leukoencephalopathy. Leukoencephalopathy is an auto-immune disease that is created by progressive damage to the white matter in the brain caused by an exposure to drugs of abuse, environmental toxins, or even chemotherapy drugs. This disease is fairly rare and often goes unreported, especially in cases resulting from drug abuse. This explained why my son was acting so strangely, the headaches and the seizure. He did not show any symptoms until several days, weeks or months after he started smoking – we weren't sure how long he had been smoking, and he wasn't coherent enough to tell us. His cognitive functions were that of a 6th grader. He was a junior in high school. This disease is rare and he needed special care.

His neurologist prescribed a treatment called IVIG, which would clean his blood of the "bad" antibodies and replace them with good ones. It would be an all-day treatment, but they were hopeful it would help him and restore him to his normal self. It was a success and he came home just before his 17th birthday. Our son was in the hospital for 19 days.

The day after Christmas, our son had another seizure. This one was worse. He had not smoked anything because I was watching him like a mother hawk guarding her nest. I was so overprotective of him. I took him back to Children's Hospital. They told me there was nothing else they could do for him and to take him back to the psychiatric hospital. I was upset. How could I take him back there when that's where he had his first seizure? I took my boy home and I stayed up with him. I prayed for him. I worshipped the Lord over him. I didn't hear from God. I knew He was there, but I didn't feel him. I felt alone, even though I knew I wasn't alone. I called one of my Sisters in Christ. It's important to have them. She told me that she would "hear" for me. She would "see" for me. She would be the arms of Christ wrapped around me. She let the love of Christ shine through her, so I could see Him working on my behalf.

The parable of the lame man, Mark 2:1-12 (NCV), explains this in such a profound way. *"A few days later, when Jesus came back to Capernaum, the news spread that he was at home. Many people gathered together so that there was no room in the house, not even outside the door. And*

Jesus was teaching them God's message. Four people came, carrying a paralyzed man. Since they could not get to Jesus because of the crowd, they dug a hole in the roof right above where he was speaking. When they got through, they lowered the mat with the paralyzed man on it. When Jesus saw the faith of these people, he said to the paralyzed man, "Young man, your sins are forgiven." Some of the teachers of the law were sitting there, thinking to themselves, "Why does this man say things like that? He is speaking as if he were God. Only God can forgive sins." Jesus knew immediately what these teachers of the law were thinking. So he said to them, "Why are you thinking these things? Which is easier: to tell this paralyzed man, "Your sins are forgiven, or to tell him, Stand up. Take your mat and walk? But I will prove to you that the Son of Man has authority on earth to forgive sins." So Jesus said to the paralyzed man, "I tell you, stand up, take your mat, and go home." Immediately the paralyzed man stood up, took his mat, and walked out while everyone was watching him. The people were amazed and praised God. They said, "We have never seen anything like this!"

    You see, you need four friends in your life to see what you can't, to – at times – carry the load for you. God never intended for any of us to live this life alone. If He did, we all wouldn't be here. The lame man had four friends to carry him to Jesus. That's what my Sister in Christ did for me. She carried me to the only One who could heal my son, heal my broken heart and restore my faith. I had others as well, praying with me, visiting with me, sharing the load at the hospital with me. If you don't have four friends you can go to, go get them. Make yourself vulnerable and accountable to four Godly women who are not afraid to step in your mess so you can grow in Christ, so you can relay the message of Jesus Christ and what He has done for you. That is what I am doing with this book. I am relaying the message that came from my mess!

After speaking with her, the Lord clearly directed my next steps. In my despair, He was in it all. I called a psychiatric hospital that was closer to our home and spoke with the intake nurse. Her name was "Lisa"... (great name). I began to tell her what had happened to my son and our family. She listened without interrupting and heard the desperation in my voice. She said to me, "Your son doesn't need to be here. You need a second opinion." I was so relieved. There was someone who believed me when I said there is something wrong with my son, he's not crazy. She said, "Why would the hospital send him to a psychiatric hospital when they treated him medically and he recovered?" That was God speaking to me. I knew God was going to heal my son. I prayed and asked God to show me the neurologist to bring him to. He did just that. I called neurologists that were listed on our insurance. I booked an appointment with the only one who actually talked to me and she could see him the next day. When we walked in, there was a plaque over the door to her office. The plaque read:

"But they that wait on the LORD shall renew their strength; they shall mount up with wings like eagles, they shall run and not be weary, They shall walk and not faint."
Isaiah 40:31 (KJV)

The Lord renewed my strength by directing my steps. It was hard to evaluate my son. I could tell the neurologist was frustrated almost as much as I, but she wasn't giving up on him. She prescribed medicine that would help him. She said rest and sleep is what heals the brain.

After about two weeks, the 2nd week of January 2015, he was much more calm. The neurologist was able to evaluate him, take more tests and confirm the diagnosis that Children's Hospital had given. I asked her and she told me emphatically that my son was NOT crazy. He was sick – medically. She ordered lots of cognitive tests, motor skills tests, tests that I cannot pronounce. He was out of school, and she predicted that he would not return for up to two years. One of the cognitive test results showed that he was at the 6th grade level. One of the motor skills test results indicated that he was at the 5th grade level. His reading was at the 3rd grade level. My son was an A/B student in High school.

I was given instruction to read to him, help him read and keep him on a routine. In addition to his resting and sleeping, all of the therapists and his neurologist were confident he would recover slowly.

As I kept praying and worshipping God, my son got better and better. He returned to school in April of that same year. He made up classes and was on track for graduation in 2016. His neurologist wasn't surprised; she served the same Almighty God. She wasn't ashamed to give him praise right there in her office.

I realized that I serve a great big God and He heard my cry. Even when I go through the darkest times of my life, *I know He is there.*

> *"Even when I walk through the darkest valley, I will not be afraid, for You are close beside me."*
> Psalms 23:4 (NLT)

8

From Mosaic to Masterpiece

Confusion can cause the inability to hear, to really listen and receive clear directions. It was only until I entered into a state of frustration that I realized I was confused.

In many areas of my life, I needed direction. At a point when I was happy with my life, I still felt unfulfilled. I had no idea what I was doing. I was busy but not accomplishing anything, just moving through life, every day, being a wife, mother, a friend, a servant in my church, using only some gifts and talents. Emptiness was a staple word that I became to accept as normal, not comfortable with it but seeing it every day in the mirror.

I have had many ideas, creative ideas, but I often felt too unprepared, unqualified or insignificant to carry out most things. These ideas were given to me by God and I had no idea what to do with them.

I prayed and I asked God in my state of frustration why I couldn't excel at any of these gifts. I asked Him, why He made me this way. He gave them to me and I couldn't seem to be successful at any of them.

The Lord spoke to me after many prayers and breakdowns. I began to see things with clarity and my gray skies became clear. He told me that I had not yet given those gifts and talents back to Him, so I would never be successful. I had given Him my life and I dedicated my life to Him, but I was still holding on to certain parts of my life. I thought I had ownership of those things. I wanted to be successful with them and I had to make those things happen.

It wasn't that I didn't want to give Him control; I just didn't realize that I hadn't done things His way. I just didn't think about giving them back to Him. I thought they were mine. When I was reminded that God's way is so much better than my way, my confusion and frustration disappeared. I wasn't too old, I wasn't too young. I wasn't inexperienced, I wasn't overqualified. I had a clear understanding that I wasn't supposed to shine my own light, but I was to reflect His light through those gifts. The Lord gave me permission to be who I was created to be. I just had to accept it.

So suddenly, the rainbow appeared. I submitted those things to God, listening for direction on only what He wanted me to do and when he wanted me to do them. I prayed and I worshiped until I heard from the voice of God.

There was finally balance. I could do one thing to the best of my ability at the right time, leaving its success in the hands of The One who makes men great at His discretion. My mosaic - the broken pieces of my life were finally creating a work of art. I will never curse my past. My past carries all the fragments that make me into a beautiful mosaic, a one-of-a-kind prize, His possession and His special treasure.

All my gifts and talents were hand-picked to create who I am. Nothing is the same – all very different, from managing an office administratively to designing and creating beautiful and tasty wedding cakes. I used to think something was wrong with me. I was overwhelmed by the number of ideas I had and all the things I could do, feeling like I could never accomplish or be successful at any of it. Here is a list of some of those gifts I have used and some things I have done:

- Event/Party Planning
- Baking

- Cooking
- Cake Decorating
- Sewing
- Writing
- Painting
- Crafts
- Violinist – Performance and Teaching
- Pianist
- Vocalist – Soloist and BGVs
- Song Writer
- Worship Leader
- Administration
- Organization
- Human Resources
- Entrepreneurship
- Bakery Owner
- Motherhood
- Sisterhood
- Wife
- Supervising
- Mentoring
- Teaching
- Sales
- Author

I am made wonderfully and in a unique fashion, for a reason but for His purpose and glory. It's His strategy. I'm different from everyone else, which makes me a weapon for the Kingdom of Heaven. I'm colorful, like a mosaic. I've been broken into many pieces to create His masterpiece. Inside me there's an abundance of ammunition to ward off the arrows of darkness to make way for the light of God. Those are His gifts "on loan" to me and I give them back to Him for His glory. Removing expectations from myself and concentrating on Jesus Christ puts everything in perspective. My focus is on pleasing Him with all that is in me.

"He gives power to the weak and strength to the powerless."
Isaiah 40:29 (NLT)

"… I am fearfully and wonderfully made."
Psalm 139:14 (KJV)

"…his treasured possession."
Deuteronomy 7:6 (NIV)

"For we are God's workmanship, created in Christ Jesus to do good works, which God prepared in advance for us to do."
Ephesians 2:10 (NIV)

9

The Mortar, My Worship

I love the way God speaks to me. It's so sweet. Even in His correction, He is so sweet to us all. Through a woman's meeting, he reminded me of the reason why He created us all, but in this instance, He wanted me to know why He created ME.

I was on a spiritual journey with these five wonderful sister friends. We were reading and studying from Rick Warren's book, "What on Earth am I Here For?" From this, I learned something that I knew, but I learned it again deeply. It took me more than 30 years to get it. God created ME to love. I was created by God and FOR God. He knew me before my parents even knew each other. I was not an accident. He had a plan for me long, long ago. He knew that I was going to feel inadequate as a teenager and through most of my adult life.

He knew that I would be so very discouraged and that I would let the words of others shape what I thought of myself. But He created ME to love, He created me especially. And He loved me so much, He sent His only Son, Jesus to die on a cross for me, to rid me of sin and to welcome me into His family. He would use those times of inadequacy for His glory and for my good. These times were fragments of something greater to come.

Now I can live a free life knowing how He feels about me and that is what is most important. Do I still think about my past and the words that were spoken over me? Of course, I do. But I am no longer captured by them. I capture every thought as the word of God instructs me to. I am no longer a slave to the power of those words. I believe what the word of God says about me and so should you.

God allowed me to experience all of that hurt, discouragement, un-acceptance, feelings of not measuring up for a deeper purpose. It was to speak to you. It was to encourage you. It was to let you know that because I made it through all of that, you can too. I didn't really know God like I do now. I did not have a long standing personal relationship with Him. God is in control of everything and nothing happens except by His permission. We have to remember that He is God.

This is why I worship the Lord. This is why I have a song in my heart every single day. This is why I write songs unto Him. He is good and He is God. He knows who I am. He created me, He has a plan for me, and I am carrying it out every day because everything works together for my good. Be encouraged, be free and know that there is no condemnation in Christ.

May the Lord make His face shine upon you, and be gracious to you; May the Lord lift up His countenance upon you and give you peace.

"For I know the plans I have for you," declares the LORD, "plans to prosper you and not to harm you, plans to give you hope and a future." Jeremiah 29:11 (NIV)

"We demolish arguments and every pretension that sets itself up against the knowledge of God, and we take captive every thought to make it obedient to Christ." II Corinthians 10:5 (NIV)

"And we know that God causes everything to work together for the good of those who love God and are called according to his purpose for them." Romans 8:28 (NLT)

"Therefore, there is now no condemnation for those who are in Christ Jesus..." Romans 8:1 (NIV)

"The LORD makes his face shine upon you and be gracious to you; the LORD turns his face toward you and gives you peace." Numbers 6:25-26 (NLT)

P.O. Box 453

Powder Springs, Georgia 30127

www.entegritypublishing.com

info@entegritypublishing.com

770.727.6517

www.ingramcontent.com/pod-product-compliance
Lightning Source LLC
Chambersburg PA
CBHW070739020526
44118CB00035B/1718